426
SERIES

I0172000

THE REASON
WHY YOU'RE HERE

Ned Erickson

Whitecaps Media
Houston, Texas
whitecapsmedia.com

The Reason: Why You're Here
© 2016 Ned Erickson
All rights reserved

ISBN: 978-1-942732-09-9

For information on bulk purchases of this book, please visit
whitecapsmedia.com

Printed in the United States of America

Table of Contents

Download the Study Guide
for this book at
whitecapsmedia.com

You Were Made For What?

Never in history has there ever been a person just like you. After God completed His finishing touches, He threw out the mold. It's true. No one will ever see the world like you do.[1] No one will hear it like you either.[2] For better or worse, each one of us will put our own unique fingerprints on this life. Your life. No one can live it for you. Others might try to look like you, act like you, and be like you—but no one can replace the original. Like a Picasso, you are one of a kind, made by the Master Himself.[3]

Think about it: God, the Master Artist, made you on purpose. There is a reason you are the way you are, and there is also a reason why you are here. Wouldn't it be great to know what the reason is? What if there was a way to find out what you were made for?

What do you think would happen if you knew, right now, the reason God placed you on this earth? Would it change the way you live? Would it influence the decisions you make? Would it influence the path you choose? You bet it would.

That's what this book is about. You and I are going to find out what we're made for. I'm not talking about predicting the future. As awesome as you might think that would be, I'm talking about something even better— I'm talking about knowing your mission in life, the one only you can complete.

Now, to accomplish this, we will need to go straight to the Source, to the Designer Himself. That's how you learn true intentions, right? If you want to know what Stonehenge was made for, ask the Druids. If you want to know what Harry Potter is about, ask J. K. Rowling. And if you want to know your purpose, ask Jesus.

Why Jesus? Because He made you. Scripture says, "For by [Jesus] all things were created, in heaven and on earth, visible and invisible . . . all things were created through him and for him" (Colossians 1:16). You see that? By Him and for Him. In a sense, it is that simple. We were made for Jesus. And just like any good creator, Jesus made you so that you would live the way you were meant to live.

"I have come," said Jesus, "that they may have life, and have it to the full."[4] Jesus came so you could become the person He created you to be. To put it another way, Jesus is, as Hebrews describes Him, "the author and perfecter of our faith."[5] Just like the author J. K. Rowling created Harry Potter, Jesus created you. And like Rowling had a higher purpose for Harry, Jesus has a higher purpose for you. The difference is Harry exists only in our imaginations—you live FOR REAL.

That's Jesus' grand purpose for you—to live for real, to be your true self.

And let me tell you, Jesus made you to be part of something huge. I promise: Life with Him is an adventure beyond what you could ever ask for or imagine. And remember this: There is no one like you, so only you can perform the part He intends you to play. Now can you see why it's so important to be your true self?

So how do you get there? How do you become the person you were created to be? It's this: You *get to know Jesus*. Wait. What? How does getting to know someone else help me become myself? Great question. Here's the answer. Because He's the Author of your life. Since before you were born, He's been crafting your story. Not only that, He is with you, right now, in it! Only He knows where your story is heading. So knowing Him is key, and what you learn about Him will make all the difference in the world. You see, as you *get to know Jesus*, the more you'll *fall in love with Him*. And the more you fall in love with Him, the more you'll *follow Him*. And the more you follow Him, the more you'll *become like Him*. And the more you become like Him, the more you *become yourself*.

Pretty straightforward.

Well, not exactly. Because what you discover as you work your way through the above progression is that you will find yourself learning new things about Jesus that will cause you to fall in love with Him in deeper ways which will lead you to follow Him into wilder places, which will transform you all over again. In other words, you don't arrive at life's answers by formula, or by going from Point A to Point B. Instead, as the writer Parker Palmer puts it, "we circle around and spiral down."[6] We become as we are becoming. That's how relationships work. And ultimately that's what Jesus most wants for you—to have a relationship with Him.

But the truth is, Jesus wants so much more for you than that! Jesus wants you to experience wholeness and healing and love and belonging. He wants you to believe that you can make a difference in this world. Maybe you think that's obvious, but a lot of what people hear about Jesus has to do with the things He *doesn't* want. Maybe all you've ever heard is that Jesus wants you to "stop this" or "wait for that," and no matter what you do, "be really serious." Well, if that's what you believe, let me be the first to tell you that's not the Jesus you will find in Scripture. The Jesus you find there is way more interested in setting people free than giving them rules to follow.[7] That's the real Jesus. That's the truth about what He wants for you. He wants things *for you*. In the coming pages we will discover some of what those things are. Not all of them. There are too many for this short study to cover! But it's a start.

So what do you say? Are you ready to find out the reason you were made?

---

[1] It's true! Your eye is as unique as your fingerprint. So in a very real sense, you see the world from a unique perspective.

[2] From http://www.yalescientific.org/2011/05/ears-the-new-fingerprints/.

[3] One of the most expensive paintings ever sold was Picasso's *Nude, Green Leaves and Bust*, which sold for over $100 million in 2010. Now, think about God, the Artist. He *created* Pablo Picasso. Just think what *His* creations (you and me) are worth!

[4] John 10:10 (NIV 1984).

[5] Hebrews 12:2 (NIV 1984).

[6] Parker Palmer, *Listen to Your Life* (San Francisco; Jossey Bass, 2000), 95.

[7] See John 8:36.

You Were Made To Be Whole

[Primary text: Mark 5:21–43]

I don't think any of us wake up in the morning intending to be someone we're not. It just sort of happens. Before we know it, we've spent too long in front of the mirror covering up our imperfections, putting "ourselves" together. We've opened the closet and slipped on the Under Armour, the hipster V-neck, the Jordans, or perhaps the goodie-two-shoes. We've walked out the door, hopped in the car, turned up the radio, and by the time we've pulled into the parking lot, we've turned into an entirely different person.

Why do we do this? Do we not like ourselves? Are we afraid others don't like us either? Well, if you're like me, the honest answer is ... Yes! Sort of. I mean, I like myself—it's just there are these things, lots of things actually, that I'd rather no one know about me.

You know what I mean? I'd rather be Mr. Perfect without even trying, but the best I've ever been able to come up with is Mr. Looks-Like-He's-Perfect. I am an impersonation. I fake it to make it. Just like you. Just like everybody. This world we live in is filled with impostors, and you and I are card-carrying practitioners.

Which is tragic, isn't it? Because like we talked about in the Introduction, never in history has there ever been a person just like you. So if you are not YOU, God misses out on the person He created you to be—you miss out on the purpose He has for you—we miss out on the blessing you were meant to be to this world. You see? We all lose when you are not yourself.

But it's hard! It's scary. Because it's one thing to be accused of something you are not—it's a whole different thing to be rejected for who you are. That's the reason for the "Under Armour." We disguise our true selves to deflect the pain and protect our hearts. Unfortunately, the disguise also prevents us from experiencing true love and being accepted for who we are.

~

One day, a huge crowd was following Jesus down the road; nothing too out of the ordinary, crowds followed Jesus pretty much wherever He went. However, this crowd was even "crowdie-er" than usual. Scripture says the crowd *pressed* around Jesus. Why? What did the crowd want to see so badly that Scripture says that people pressed around Him? Well, there was someone with Jesus, a guy by the name of Jairus, who just so happened to be one of the most powerful people in the country. He had come to Jesus because his daughter was dying, and Jesus had agreed to heal her. No one wanted to miss that.

So down the road they went, Jairus, Jesus, and the crowd. Nothing out of the ordinary. Just another day in the life of Jesus. That is, until something unexpected happened ...

A woman pushed her way through the crowd and touched Jesus' clothes. Why would she do that? Well, it wasn't because she was a member of the fashion police. The reality was she was at the end of her rope.

Scripture tells us the woman "had had a discharge of blood for twelve years, and [she] had suffered much under many physicians, and had spent all that she had, and was no better but rather grew worse."[1]

This bleeding was the kind of bleeding women have every month. But instead of stopping, hers kept going. Can you imagine how awful that would be? But that wasn't the worst of it. Her condition had made her an outcast. In that culture, a woman like that couldn't be in contact with anyone. There was an actual law about it (you can look it up in Leviticus 15:25). Basically, a woman had to separate herself from others for as long as her period was happening. Hers hadn't stopped *for twelve years*. She couldn't have relationships; she couldn't participate in society. And it had been that way for more than a decade! She had sought the help of doctors, but they had only made the bleeding worse (all the while bleeding her of money). She had nothing left. She had no other options, except ... she had heard about this man, this healer named Jesus. We don't know if she lived nearby or if she had traveled a hundred miles. All we know is that she had made up her mind; she was touching His clothes. She didn't want to disturb Him. Jesus probably had better things to do, like heal this important guy's daughter. But maybe. Maybe if she touched His clothes, just the hem of His cloak, then maybe, maybe that would be enough of Jesus to heal her.

So she did. She touched the hem of His cloak. And "immediately her bleeding stopped."[2] Her plan worked.

She had gotten her miracle; now, all she had to do was slip back into the crowd, back to her invisible life …

… only Jesus didn't let her! "Who touched my clothes?" He asked. The disciples looked at one another and shrugged because hundreds of people had been pressing against Him. "But Jesus," the Scriptures tell us, "kept looking around to see who had done it."[3]

Now, think about what must have been going through the woman's mind. No doubt she was terrified. She had stolen some of Jesus' power, and He knew it. What if He asked for it back? (Could He do that?) What if He *un*-healed her? (Could He do that?) But those were only two of her problems. What if the woman had taken the power that was meant for the dying girl? What if the girl died? What would the crowd do to her then? What about Jairus? He had the power to ruin her life.

Well, to her dismay, it was obvious Jesus wasn't going to stop searching the crowd until He found her. Like it or not, there was nothing to do but confess. And so she "came in fear and trembling and fell down before him and told him the whole truth."[4] Now, Scripture doesn't go into detail, but what I think it means when it says that she told Him *the whole truth* is that she told Him the WHOLE TRUTH. In other words, she spilled out her guts: the bleeding, the doctors, the money, the pain, the anger, the despair, the loss, the twelve years of emotional and physical suffering, the twelve years of God not listening to her prayers—she told Jesus all of it. I love how J. B. Phillips translated this verse: "[she] flung herself before him and told him the whole story."[5] Every part. And guess what Jesus did: He listened.

Can you imagine the scene? The crowd, the disciples, Jairus—they all had their own agendas and expectations. The crowd, I'm sure, was growing impatient. I picture a wisecracker a few rows back, shouting: "Hey, what's the hold up?" Others probably turned around and went home. But Jesus listened to the woman's whole story. Then, there were the disciples. They were probably frustrated. Here was Jairus, the powerful synagogue ruler. He could give Jesus support among the other religious leaders. In fact, if he got behind their cause, Jairus might be able to bankroll the entire mission. With a man like him, Jesus could become the most famous person in Israel. All Jesus had to do was heal his daughter. But Jesus listened to the woman's whole story. All the while, Jairus helplessly stood there while his daughter was dying, while Jesus wasted precious time on a woman who had already been healed. "Get your priorities straight, Jesus. My daughter is dying!" he must have thought to himself. In fact, at that very moment, men were coming from Jairus' house—and it didn't look like they were coming with good news. More on that in a minute.

Jairus' daughter would have to wait. Jesus was caring for someone else—a nobody.

You know, you might think that God doesn't have time to listen to you. Or maybe you think what you have to say isn't important enough for Him to listen. Well, if you get anything from watching Jesus, it's that Jesus makes time. If you want to tell Him your story, He will listen to the whole darn thing!

Finally, only after she was done, Jesus said to the woman, "Daughter ..." *Daughter!* Can you imagine how much that one word must have meant to this woman? She had lost everything. She had nobody, not a penny to her name—and here was Jesus saying that from now on she could consider herself part of His family. Wow! Who knows how long it had been since this woman had heard such tenderhearted words? We do know it is the first time in the Gospel of Mark that Jesus says such a thing. *Daughter.* From now on you are family. "Your faith has made you well; go in peace, and be healed of your disease."[6]

Now, pay attention because this is significant. Do you see what Jesus did? He separated wellness from

17

healing. "Go in peace, and be healed of your disease," He said. That part is obvious—the healing happened when she touched Jesus' clothes. But what about wellness, or "wholeness" as the King James Version translates it? The original word in Greek is the word *sozo*, which is most often translated *to save*. Jesus was pointing out to the woman that He had given her not one, but two miracles. The first was healing. The second was wholeness. And of the two, wholeness was the one that saved her. And when did the second miracle take place? When He listened to her whole story.

Healing and Wholeness: There's a difference, isn't there? One addresses a specific need; the other impacts an entire life. That's what Jesus is after— He's after you—all of you. Jesus did not come just to heal you or forgive you; He came to make you whole. Sociologist Dr. Brené Brown defines wholeness this way: "Wholehearted living is about engaging in our lives from a place of worthiness."[7]

And where do we get this worthiness from? Well, the best place, and really the only place that lasts, is from the One who made you.

Jesus said this once about the ones He made, "The kingdom of heaven is like treasure hidden in a field, which a man found and covered up. Then in his joy he goes and sells all that he has and buys that field."[8]

This is what Bible scholars call a parable—it's a story with a purpose. So what's Jesus' purpose? What's the treasure? Jesus says it's "the kingdom of heaven." What's the kingdom of heaven? It's the way things were meant to be, that universe God designed way back in the beginning. And to Him it was so valuable that in His joy He sold all He had. Scripture puts it this way: "For the *joy* set before [Jesus] [he] endured the cross, scorning its shame."[9] You see, to Jesus, it was worth enduring the cross to get His kingdom back, even if it cost Him all He had. And what did He get for paying the price? The treasure. And guess who is included in that treasure? YOU.

You are God's treasure. And you were so valuable to Him He gave *all He had* to get *you* back. You get that? It cost Jesus everything. *He died.* But there's more. Jesus didn't merely die to *sozo* (save) you. He died to make you whole. Why? Because to Him, you were worth it. He actually considers your heart prime real estate! You heard me. Jesus, the Creator of the Universe, could live anywhere He wants, but where He *chooses* to live is in your heart!

In a very true sense, you are God's one and only. And you know what we call one-and-only things? We call them priceless. We call them treasures. That's what you are. Now, you might not look like one. Your face might have pimples and your feet might stink and that cowlick in your hair might never go away, but the fact remains the same: You are priceless, my friend. The truth about you is you're worth a King's ransom. And if you have a problem with me saying this about you, take it up with the God. He proved it by sacrificing His Son for you.

Why? Because you're worth it. Jesus came to make you whole, and wholehearted living is about engaging life from a place of worthiness.

Well, that's great, Ned. The bleeding woman got her life back, but what about the girl? What about Jairus' daughter? She died. Jesus let her die.

You're right. He did.

I can only imagine what feelings must have been going through Jairus at that moment. Shock. Grief. Horror. I'm sure he was angry. He was a synagogue ruler, after all, and here was this supposed "Son of God" choosing an outcast over his daughter. I wouldn't have blamed Jairus if he had punched Jesus in the face.

But then this happened: "Overhearing what they said, Jesus said to [Jairus], 'Do not fear, only believe'"

(Mark 5:36). And for some reason, Jairus did. At least, he believed enough to let Jesus into his house. Leaving the crowd at the door, Jesus, a few disciples, Jairus, and his wife went inside, down the hall, up the stairs. Behind them, they could hear the servants laughing. The girl was beyond healing. Jesus was about to make a fool of Himself and their master. Jesus ignored them. He reassured Jairus. He shut the door to the room. Jairus, his wife, and the disciples looked on as Jesus went to the child. Her young face was gray, her chest unmoving. Jesus knelt beside her. He took her hand and said to her, "Little girl, I say to you, arise."[10]

And she did.

Jairus' daughter came back to life. She was twelve years old. Did you catch that detail? The girl was twelve years old, the same number of years as the woman with the bleeding suffered. Two daughters, twelve years—neither was more important than the other because both were infinitely important to Jesus. They both mattered to Him, and that day, Jesus had given both of them new life.

That's my Jesus. The giver-backer of life. That's the reason He came—to give us life, to make us whole. You see, Jesus is not interested in patching up our problems or duct-taping our dilemmas. He's after total restoration—making broken things new, empty things full, lost things found, and dead things alive!

You heard me right. Jesus can bring even dead things to life. He proved it to Jairus. And later, He proved it again by coming back to life Himself!

---

[1] Mark 5:25–26.

[2] Mark 5:29 (NIV 1984)

[3] Mark 5:32 (NIV 1984).

[4] Mark 5:33.

[5] Mark 5:33 (PHILLIPS).

[6] Mark 5:34.

[7] Brené Brown, *Daring Greatly* (New York, New York; Gotham Books, 2012), 9.

[8] Matthew 13:44.

[9] Hebrews 12:2 (NIV 1984), emphasis added.

[10] Mark 5:41.

You Were Made To Belong

[Primary text: John 4:5–26]

She had a hard life. True, a lot of the hard in her life was her own fault. But that didn't diminish the fact; all that did was clarify it. The same is true for all of us. Wherever we find ourselves, there are reasons for how we got there. Maybe hers was that she hadn't been given enough attention by her father. Maybe she had been abused as a child. Maybe she was just a victim of circumstance. Maybe she wasn't. We don't know.

The only information Scripture gives us is that she was drawing water from a well by herself in the middle of the day. What can we learn from a detail like that? Well, for one, she must have needed water, and when one needs such a thing one goes to a well. But why the middle of the day? Most performed this chore in the morning or evening when it wasn't so hot. Most women went in groups. They used it as an excuse to hang out with their friends and catch up on the latest gossip. This woman came in the heat of the day *when no one was there*. Why? She must not have wanted to be with the others. Or was the opposite true? Did the others not want to be with her?

Except *that day she wasn't alone*. A man was there.

"Will you give me a drink?" he asked her.

The woman cocked her head to the side. *Doesn't this man know it's not appropriate to associate with a woman in public?* she thought to herself. *He should. He looks Jewish. No respectable Jew would do such a thing, especially with a mixed-race Samaritan like me. Or maybe this Jew isn't the respectable type.*

She decided to test him. "How is it that you, a Jew, ask for a drink from me, a woman of Samaria?"[1]

The man answered, "If you knew the gift of God, and who it is that is saying to you, 'Give me a drink,' you would have asked him, and he would have given you living water."[2]

Now the woman was really confused. *Clearly, this man seems to be after something more than a drink. Then again, men usually are. But this man doesn't look to me like he's flirting.*

"Sir," she said, playing it cool, "you have nothing to draw water with, and the well is deep. Where do you get that living water?"[3]

"Everyone who drinks of this water will be thirsty again, but whoever drinks of the water that I will give him will never be thirsty again," the man quipped.[4]

Who does this guy think he is? A magician? "Sir," she said, calling his bluff, "give me this water, so that I will not be thirsty or have to come here to draw water."[5] *There. That'll show him who he is messing with.*

"Go, call your husband, and come back," replied the man.[6]

You could almost hear the needle screech across the record. *Call your husband? How did he know?* The woman swallowed down the lump rising in her throat. Up to this point, she thought she had the upper hand. After all, he was thirsty; she had the bucket. All of the sudden, she wasn't so sure. "I have no husband," she said, her voice cracking.

"You are right in saying, 'I have no husband,'" said the man, "for you have had five husbands, and the one you now have is not your husband."[7]

She staggered slightly as blood rushed to her cheeks. The bucket shook from the quivering in her fingers. This woman was not one to be caught off-guard. But this man seemed to know her deepest darkest secrets. Five men she had married. Five men she had left. And the man she was with now she had stolen from somebody else. How this man deciphered this information she hadn't a clue. But she was certain he now understood the reason she had come to fetch water in the middle of the day. To put it bluntly: She was the town tramp. Women hated her; men only liked her for her body. She was damaged goods. And when it came down to it, she'd rather suffer from the heat than suffer people's judgmental glares and venomous whispers.

Now here was this stranger *who knew everything about her.* In a single sentence, he had cut through the layers and exposed the very worst thing about her. Yet there was no judgment in his voice. Her licentious immorality didn't seem to bother him one bit. So why bring it up? Why choose to humiliate her like this? Didn't he care about her? Or was that the point—*did he really care about her?* At the moment, all she knew was that *she had never met a man like this before.*

Feeling uncomfortable, the woman decided to change the subject. "Sir, I perceive that you are a prophet. Our fathers worshipped on this mountain, but you say that in Jerusalem is the place where people ought to worship."[8]

Huh? What is she talking about? A little context might help. Back then, Jews believed that the temple in Jerusalem was the only place a person could go to properly worship God. Because of the woman's ethnicity, she and her people were forbidden to go to Jerusalem and worship there. So these people, the Samaritans, had built their own temple, an act that made the Jews hate them even more.

Jesus (if you haven't figured it out, He's the man in the story) took her change of subject in stride. "The hour is coming, and is now here," He said, not missing a beat, "when the true worshipers will worship the Father in spirit and truth, for the Father is seeking such people to worship him."⁹ My translation: "When it comes to worship, God is not interested in your location; He is interested in your heart."

I like the way John Eldridge, the author of *Wild at Heart*, explains the meaning of the word *heart* in Scripture. Though Jesus does not use the word here, what He is getting at by saying "spirit and truth" is really the same thing. Here is Eldridge:

> "Heart in Scripture," notes Charles Ryrie, "is considered the very center and core of life." That's right. The heart is the deep center of our life. "The innermost

part of the human personality," says James Houston, "the center of those qualities that make us human." Yes, that's it. The heart is who we are. The real self. I think I like Oswald Chamber's definition most: "The use of the Bible term *heart* is best understood by simply saying 'me.' Me ... My heart is me. The real me. Your heart is you. The deepest, truest you."[10]

"God is spirit," Jesus continued, "and those who worship him must worship in spirit and truth."[11] Replace "spirit and truth" with heart, and it makes sense. God's worshippers must worship from the heart—from who they are. *Listen!* Jesus is saying, *God isn't looking for perfect people; He's looking for AUTHENTIC PEOPLE. Don't come to me as you think you should be. Come to me as you are.*

Did you hear that? God wants—no, He *insists*—that you come one way and one way only: just the way you are, warts and all.

This had to be the strangest conversation this woman had ever been a part of. From water to infidelity to God to the nature of worship—this might well be one of the strangest conversations in history. I love how Jesus is so comfortable throughout it. It's like He could talk to you about anything (something to think about!).

I have no doubt this woman was moved by Jesus. He knew everything about her and accepted her anyway. He loved her in a way she had never known—and you would think this woman would know! She had more "lovers" than anyone. But Jesus' love was different. His love was generous with no strings attached and no agenda but authenticity.

Suddenly, she discovered the roles had been reversed. He wasn't thirsty—she was. After years of misuse and abuse, the well of her heart had become dry. She had tried to fill it with men, replacing physical affection for true love, and it was like drinking ocean water, leaving her thirstier than before. *Yes*, she thought, *I am the thirsty one*. And here before her was a man, a bucketless man, offering to fill her with the water of a love that would never go away. And for some reason she believed him.

"I know that Messiah is coming (he who is called Christ). When he comes, he will tell us all things."[12] The words surprised her as they passed through her lips. She was not religious. She had never said words like this before. And yet deep in her soul, she sensed she had been crying for a savior every day of her life.

"I who speak to you am he," Jesus said with a smile.

John 4:26. Look it up. It's the first time in the Gospel of John that Jesus reveals to somebody His true identity. And who does He tell? A king? A priest? His disciples? No. He tells a mixed-race, mixed-up, messed up, and utterly despised woman.

~

One time Jesus was being ridiculed for the people He hung out with. He replied, "Those who are well have no need of a physician, but those who are sick. I came not to call the righteous, but sinners."[13] Jesus was being ironic here because He really came for everybody. But Jesus couldn't really help people unless they were willing to admit they needed it. Sinners, therefore, had one thing that the "righteous" people didn't: They *knew* they were screwed up. The irony is that the people ridiculing Jesus were sinners, too; they just weren't ready to admit it. They were like people with cancer who didn't know they had cancer, and you know what happens to people like that? *They die.*

Only after cancer is diagnosed can the right course of action be undertaken. That is why vulnerability with God is so important. He will not heal what remains unrevealed. In the above story, Jesus wasn't able to fill this woman with the living water of acceptance until she was willing to admit she was empty.

Renowned psychologist Dr. David Brenner said this: "Love is transformational only when it is received in vulnerability."[14]

In other words, Jesus will only be able to transform the REAL YOU when you are real with Him.

But did you notice that Jesus was also real with her? Honesty went both ways. That is the nature of acceptance: me being ME, you being YOU, then connecting the two with love.

John Eldridge says this about Jesus: "Christ did not die for an idea. He died for a person, and that person is you."[15]

Jesus loves YOU. That's the honest to God truth, and you don't need to change a thing to receive it. The fact is, without God you can't change. And while we are on the subject, you want to know the truth about change? It's the love of Jesus that changes you!

Scripture says this: "Yet to all who received [Jesus], to those who believed in his name, he gave the right to become children of God."[16] When you receive God's love, you become a member of His family, and with membership come all the rights and privileges thereof. See, there is one distinction between a friend and a family member. You can un-friend a friend, but you can't un-family a family member (though sometimes my daughter wishes she could do so to her little brother!) The point is when you accept Jesus, or better put, when you accept Jesus' acceptance of you, you belong.

Brené Brown in her excellent book *Daring Greatly* reflects on a series of interviews she had with a group of eighth-graders.

> When I asked [them] to break into small teams and come up with the difference between *fitting in* and *belonging*, their answers floored me:
>
> *Belonging* is being somewhere where you want to be, and they want you. *Fitting in* is being somewhere you really want to be, but they don't care one way or the other.
>
> Belonging is being accepted for you. *Fitting in* is being accepted for being like everybody else. I get to be me if I belong. I have be like you to fit in.[17]

It is easy to get tricked into thinking that Jesus wants us to "fit in," that Jesus wants to come into our hearts and minds in order to reprogram us into these perfect little followers. That is what it means to be a Christian, right? To be like Jesus? At least, that is what good Christians are like. You go to church and everyone looks the same. They all vote for the same political candidates. They are anti-this and pro-that. They "love" the sinner, but "hate" the sin. They don't realize how judgmental that really is. They're too busy trying to look better than everybody else.

Well, that's not what Jesus is after at all. Jesus came to give you a place where you can *belong*. To use the eighth graders' words, Jesus accepts you for being you. He doesn't ask you to be like everybody else. He doesn't want you to be anybody but yourself.

I love the way Jesus works. He sees through our masks, past our junk. He even sees past the sin that caused the junk. He looks past it all until He sees YOU. The REAL YOU. That's what Jesus does. He gives worth to the worthless, He notices the overlooked, He dignifies the undignified, and He does extraordinary things through the most ordinary of individuals.

In one conversation, Jesus changed this woman's life forever. How did He do it? He loved her the way she was, and that love changed her. Of course it changed her. Love like that can change the world.

It certainly changed her world.

You won't believe this. But this woman by the well, the one who woke up that morning planning to avoid everybody, guess what she does? She leaves her bucket, goes back to town, and tells everyone she meets about the Person she just met. And then guess what happens? "Many Samaritans from that town believed in [Jesus] because of the woman's testimony, 'He told me all that I ever did.'"[18] You get that? She came out of hiding ("He told all that I ever did"). She owned her mess. And her honesty about her brokenness changed a city.

The same could happen in the places we live. However, your world won't change much with your poor attempts at perfection. Looking like a "good little Christian" might get you a gold star from your Sunday school teacher, but it will not make a difference in the great grand scheme of things. On the other hand, honesty will. That was all Jesus asked from this woman, and that is really all that He is asking from you. And what does He give you in return? He gives you the living water your dried-up well of a heart is longing for— love, acceptance, and a place to belong. With water like that, you may never thirst again.

---

[1] John 4:9.

[2] John 4:10.

[3] John 4:11.

[4] John 4:13–14.

[5] John 4:15.

[6] John 4:16 (NIV 1984).

[7] John 4:17–18.

[8] John 4:19–20.

[9] John 4:23–24.

[10] John Eldridge, *Waking the Dead* (Nashville; Nelson, 2003), 49–50.

[11] John 4:24.

[12] John 4:25.

[13] Mark 2:17.

[14] David Brenner, *Surrender to Love* (Downers Grove; IVP Books, 2003), 76–77.

[15] Eldridge, 50.

[16] John 1:12 (NIV 1984).

[17] Brené Brown, *Daring Greatly*, 232.

[18] John 4:39.

You Were Made To Be Loved

[Primary text: Luke 15:11–32]

Pews are filled with men and women in their finest regalia. Organ music wafts through the rafters with exultant jubilee. Expectancy pulses from one person to another as the priest, his arms wide open, turns to welcome the prince and princess. He beckons them to the altar then clasps his hands together as the organ pipes its final note.

The church is so silent you can hear a pin drop as the priest scans the audience with eyes that could stare down a rhinoceros, and begins: "Mawage. Mawage is wot bwings us togevver tooday. Mawage, that bwessed awangment, that dweam wifin a dweam …"[1]

What? You didn't know I was talking about *The Princess Bride*? Ha! I love that movie: the story of a hero who does whatever it takes to win back his true love.

After Buttercup loses hope that Wesley will ever return for her, she agrees to marry the selfish and conceited Prince Humperdinck. Meanwhile, Wesley, who didn't return because he had been captured by pirates, has survived years of indentured labor, scaled the cliffs of insanity, fought an ambidextrous swordsman, battled giants, drunk poison, fended off rodents of unusual size, suffered "The Machine" in the Pit of Despair, and died (OK, he mostly died), only to come back and rescue his lost love from the hands of the evil prince.

Remind you of anything?

It should. Because as amazing as the love story is between Wesley and Buttercup, it is merely an echo of a greater one. It's a tale about a person who gets fooled into thinking that her true love isn't trustworthy, so she goes her own way and gets mixed up in all kinds of bad things. Little does she know that her love is coming after her the whole time. And like Wesley, the hero in this story endures some seriously harrowing adventures. He battles demons, escapes death multiple times, withstands the schemes of a villain once called the Lord of the Flies, suffers under the brutal mechanisms of a ruthless empire, and dies (all the way), only to come back to life and rescue His lost love from the shackles of the evil villain. Who is this hero? Jesus, of course. And who is His true love? You!

Did you know that Jesus actually describes you as His fiancée?[2] For us guys (and maybe also for you girls) that might feel a bit weird. But think about it for a second. Jesus, the Crown Prince of the Universe, loves the people of this world so much that the closest comparison He can come up with is the love a guy has for the woman he wants to marry. If that's not crazy, think about this: When we sinned—or cheated on Him, you could say—He didn't renege on "the proposal." Instead, He went into enemy territory, knowing full well that the price for winning His beloved back was His very own life. That's right, Jesus volunteered to be tortured to death for you. In fact, He died at the hands of the very people He came to save. Romans 5:10 puts it this way: "When we were God's enemies, we were reconciled to him through the death of his Son" (NIV 1984). Wow! That's crazy love.

Why would Jesus do that? I mean, why would He do that *for me*? That is a great question. And the only reason I can give you is the answer that God gives: *He loves you.* He loved you enough to die for you, and He loves you so much He wants you to be in His family. In fact, He loves you *so much* He put His very self inside you. I'm not exaggerating. The truth is Jesus loves you so completely that He wants to spend every day from now through eternity with you. Wow. That's some serious commitment. And that's all the reason He gives for doing all He does for us. The question for you and me is whether or not we are willing to receive it.

Receiving is important. Have you ever received the "dead fish" handshake? Or have you ever hugged someone who hugs like they think you might have some contagious disease (maybe that's just me). The point is that a handshake and a hug take two to work. The same is true with relationships, and a relationship with Jesus is no different. He can love you all He wants, but He can't have a relationship with you unless you are willing to love Him back.

∼

The most famous story Jesus ever told is called "The Parable of the Prodigal Son." In the story there is a father who has two sons. The older one is responsible. The younger one is prodigal, which means "extravagantly wasteful." This prodigal son shows his *prodigal-ness* in that he asks his father for his entire inheritance—before his father is dead!—then goes to a foreign country with the money and spends it all on what Jesus describes as "wild living." That *is* wasteful, if you ask me.

What would make a person do such a thing? You would think that maybe his decision had something to do with his relationship with his father. Did the two not get along? What's strange is that the word the son uses when asking for his inheritance is actually a term of endearment, something along the lines of "Daddy." When you think about it, the son would not have requested such an outlandish thing if he didn't believe his father would give it to him. All signs point to a loving father. So what was it that made the prodigal leave? It's hard to say, except I totally understand. Like the prodigal, I have a loving father in God. And yet, it is so tempting to do what I want to do instead of what He wants me to do. I know being close to Him is right and good; nevertheless I volunteer to run away. I can't exactly explain why I do it. It just seems better at the time. Wild living looks so fun. And I have this unquenchable fear of missing out. I feel restless "at home." And so, like the prodigal, I take all the stuff God has given me (life, talent, opportunity, etc.) and run.

And just like what happens to the prodigal, eventually the fun runs out.

"And when he had spent everything ... he began to be in need. So he went and hired himself out to one of the citizens of that country, who sent him into his fields to feed pigs. And he was longing to be fed with the pods that the pigs ate, and no one gave him anything."[3]

Abandoned, hungry, penniless, and lost—the prodigal finally hits rock bottom. All he has to his name is that ... *his name.* Turns out that's a lot.

The story continues: "When he came to his senses, he said ... 'I will set out and go back to my father.'"[4] Notice that the prodigal son does not say "go back home." Instead, he says, "go back to my father." Instinctively, he knows that even though he told his father that he wished him dead, he believes that the father still loves him.

Maybe you have that instinct, too, about God. Maybe you don't. Maybe like the prodigal, your restlessness has led you to places you are ashamed to have found yourself in. But what if your restlessness is actually *your Father's voice calling you home*? Seventeen hundred years ago, St. Augustine said as much. "Our hearts," he said, "are restless until they find rest in God."[5] In other words, restlessness is a gift. It's a dangerous gift because it can lead us to foreign lands and wild living, but it's also the voice that can lead us back home. *Maybe it's time for you to listen to the restlessness you feel and do what the prodigal does.* He returns.

What about you? Are you ready to return?

Now, this is the place in the story where the people listening to Jesus began to feel uncomfortable. See if you can figure out why. "But while [the son] was still a long way off, his father saw him and felt compassion, and ran and embraced him and kissed him."[6]

The father saw him while the son was still a long way off. You get that? The father must have been looking for him. You can imagine him sitting on the porch every day, scanning the hills for the tiniest of human blips on the horizon. Finally, one appears, and the father *runs.* In that culture, it would have been unheard of to see a father run, period, but especially to run toward a son who had shamed his family by wishing his father dead! Yet that is what this father does. He runs. He humiliates himself in front of the entire village, but he doesn't care. His son is back, and he refuses to be apart from him a minute longer.

He doesn't even let the son finish his "I'm sorry" speech. Interrupting him, the father shouts to his servants, "Quick! Bring the best robe and put it on him. Put a ring on his finger and sandals on his feet. Bring the fattened calf and kill it. Let's have a feast and celebrate.

For this son of mine was dead and is alive again."[7] You see that? In one fell swoop, the father restores his son into the family. All that's left to do is party.

Happy ending ... if only the story ended there. Remember at the beginning? The father had *two* sons.[8] What's the other one doing? We find out in verse 25: He's in the field, working. While the younger one is in a foreign land wasting his father's money, this older son never leaves home. He's a good boy. He does what he is supposed to do. He works hard. For all appearances, the son has it all together. So it seems on the outside. However, soon we see that underneath his perfect-son façade there is a heart just as lost as his brother's.

When the elder brother heard the music and learned that it was for his younger brother, "the older brother became angry and refused to go in."[9] Why? Well, it's understandable, isn't it? His father isn't treating him fairly. He spells it out in the next few lines:

> "Look, these many years I have served you, and I never disobeyed your command, yet you never gave me a young goat, that I might celebrate with my friends. But when this son of yours came, who has devoured your property with prostitutes, you killed the fattened calf for him!"[10]

I totally get the elder son's reaction. Maybe some of you do, too. Like him, maybe you haven't squandered your God-given gifts on wild living. Maybe you work hard at being good. Maybe you think it's unfair that God treats everyone the same. Maybe you feel like good behavior should be rewarded. That seems right, doesn't it? Doesn't God want to reward us for doing the right thing? The elder son feels this way. *I've slaved for you*, one translation puts it. You see that? The elder son stayed at home, he did all the right things, but he feels like a slave. Do you feel this way sometimes? Do you feel like being a Christian is hard work? Does it make you mad when people don't get what they deserve? Including you? Shouldn't you be rewarded for being such a good person? If we're honest, there's a little bit of "elder son" in all of us.

Clearly, something is broken in the relationship between this son and his father. However, it's not the father's love. Notice: Just as the father runs to the younger son, the father *goes* to the elder one.[11] Again, in this culture a host leaving his own party to deal with a party-pooper older son would be absolutely humiliating. Yet, listen to the kindness in how the father treats the elder son: "My son," the father says, "you are always with me, and everything I have is yours."[12] How amazing is the father's love here? Just like the father did with the younger son, he gives the elder son more than he deserves. *Everything I have is yours,* he says. "We had to celebrate and be glad, because this brother of yours was dead and is alive again; he was lost and is found."[13]

That is where the parable ends. We don't know if the elder son goes to the party. We don't know if the younger son screws up again. But we can be pretty sure that the father will never give up on either of them.

Likewise, your heavenly Father will never give up on you. Think about this: If anyone is "extravagantly wasteful" in this story, it's the father with his love. This "prodigal father" gives love freely, often, and at great expense to himself. And that was the main thing Jesus was trying to get across—the enormity of God's love to a people who don't deserve it.

Back to the original question: are we willing to receive it?

Repentance is a word you might have heard before. It literally means "to turn from" or "to change one's mind." And usually when you hear someone talking about this passage, he or she will point to the part when the younger son "came to his senses" as the moment the younger son "repents." But that is not how the people of Jesus' day would have understood it.

Biblical and Middle Eastern scholar Kenneth E. Bailey spent twenty years living with a group of people called the Bedouin. They are a nomadic tribe whose culture has not changed very much over the last two thousand years. That was what intrigued Bailey. These people were like the people Jesus would have talked to. So Bailey had this idea that they might have a more accurate understanding of the stories Jesus told.[14]

Their reaction to the prodigal son story was astonishing to him. The Bedouin helped Bailey understand the scandalous nature of the younger son's "rebellion," the disgraceful actions of "the father who ran," and the shameful disrespect the elder brother displayed by not attending the brother's party. However, what surprised Bailey most was the Bedouins' concept of repentance. To them, repentance did not happen the moment the younger son "came to his senses." Instead, repentance happened when the son *received the father's embrace.*

In the Bedouin culture (and Jesus' culture), the father could hold onto the son until the cows came home, but their relationship would not be restored until the son hugged him back.

The same is true for you and me.

God's love is constant. He cannot love us any more, and He refuses to loves us any less than He already does. In other words, we can wiggle and writhe out of God's embrace, but it will never change the way He feels about us. His arms are always reaching out to us. The decision we have to make is whether to embrace Him back.

You see *that* was what we were made for. We were made to be in a relationship with God, made to be able to say as the bride says to Solomon: "I am my beloved's and my beloved is mine" (Song of Solomon 6:3). Put simply: You and I were made to be loved.

I love the movie *Hitch*. Hitch (played by Will Smith) is a relationship expert who makes his living by helping guys like Albert (Kevin James) win the girls of their dreams. One day, Hitch is teaching Albert the best way to kiss.

> HITCH: This is what most guys do. They rush in to take the kiss. But you're not most guys. See, the secret to a kiss is to go 90% of the way ... and then hold.
>
> ALBERT: For how long?
>
> HITCH: As long as it takes for her to come the other 10%.[15]

Do you get the picture? It's not a perfect analogy, but the secret to a kiss is the same secret to any relationship. It takes two. God, the Prodigal Father, has done everything in His power. He has gone more than 90% of the way. But for you to experience the love He made you to experience, you're going to have to make a move toward Him. Yes, for you to be loved—for you to know the unconditional, everlasting embrace of God—you have to embrace Him back.

So how do you do that? How do you hug someone who is invisible? That's a great question. It begins with a word, the same word that I longed to hear from my girlfriend, Lia, when I proposed to her on February 8, 2000: "Yes." Jesus wants to hear you say *yes* to Him. And when you do it's like putting on the engagement ring. It's like believing in a promise. For richer and poorer. For better and worse. And not even in death will you be apart. That is God's love. And if we say yes to Him, this is the promise He keeps—that one day, you and I, God's loved ones, will experience a wedding reception that never ends, an everlasting party with our Bridegroom, the Son of God, whose love for you will never fade, never waver, and never go away.

---

[1] *The Princess Bride* (20th Century Fox, 1987).

[2] In Matthew 9:15 Jesus calls Himself the "bridegroom." Heaven is described as a wedding feast where Jesus is the groom and we are the bride (Revelation 21:2). The analogy is used several times as well in the Old Testament (see Isaiah 54:6 and 62:5; Ezekiel 16:7–14; and basically the entire book of Hosea).

[3] Luke 15:14–16.

[4] Luke 15:17 (NIV 1984).

[5] Augustine of Hippo, *Confessions*, public domain.

[6] Luke 15:20.

[7] Luke 15:22–24 (NIV 1984).

[8] See Luke 15:11.

[9] Luke 15:28 (NIV 1984).

[10] Luke 15:29–30.

[11] See Luke 15:28.

[12] Luke 15:31–32 (NIV 1984).

[13] Luke 15:32 (NIV 1984).

[14] See Kenneth Bailey, *The Cross and the Prodigal: Luke 15 Through the Eyes of Middle Eastern Peasants* (Downer's Grove; IVP, 2005).

[15] *Hitch* (Sony Pictures, 2005).

You Were Made To Be Free

[Primary text: Mark 4:35—5:20]

Théoden was the King of Rohan, a kingdom known for its horses and the bravery of its warriors. He was their leader, a heroic man, known for his generosity. Sadly, his life had taken a devastating turn when his chief advisor, Gríma (or Wormtongue as many called him) turned on Théoden and plotted to destroy him.

With meticulous precision Wormtongue poisoned Théoden. Literally, he poisoned him. But worse to Théoden's well-being was the poison of Wormtongue's lies. *You are old; you are weak; you are dying*, he would tell the king. And by the time Gandalf the great wizard reached Théoden's Golden Hall in J. R. R. Tolkien's second book of the *Lord of the Rings* trilogy, Théoden had become a shell of the man he once was. As Tolkien described it, he "was so bent with age that he seemed almost a dwarf."[1] Théoden had literally become half the person he once was, so stunted he had become mute. He no longer could speak for himself, not because he had lost his voice, but because Wormtongue had taken his confidence to use it. Crippled by lies, the once great king had become overruled with fear and self-doubt. He was at the mercy of his advisor.

And Wormtongue used his power to great, personal advantage. He was a namer, defining realities for others. Listen to the way he speaks to Gandalf:

> "Why indeed should we welcome you, Master Stormcrow? *Láthspell* I name you, Ill-news; and ill news is an ill guest they say." He laughed grimly, as he lifted his heavy eyelids for a moment and gazed on the strangers with dark eyes.[2]

Stormcrow? Ill-news? Doesn't Wormtongue know to whom he's talking? That's the point. Gandalf was the greatest sorcerer in Middle Earth. The only way Wormtongue had a chance against him was if he could convince Gandalf to believe that he was merely a cranky old crow. If Gandalf fell for it, he would become his own undoing. Unfortunately for Wormtongue, Gandalf had a firm understanding of who he was. He refused to believe the lies. And before Wormtongue could do a thing about it, Gandalf had gone all Middle Earth on him!

Casting his tattered cloak to the side, Gandalf spoke in a clear cold voice:

"The wise speak only of what they know, Gríma son of Gálmód. A witless worm have you become. Therefore be silent, and keep your forked tongue behind your teeth . . ."

He raised his staff. There was a roll of thunder. The sunlight was blotted out from the eastern windows; the whole hall became suddenly dark as night. The fire faded into sullen embers. Only Gandalf could be seen, standing white and tall before the blackened hearth . . . Wormtongue sprawled on his face.[3]

Whether or not you have read the *Lord of the Rings* books or watched all eleven-plus hours of movies, I hope you get the picture. One of the most deadly forces in this world is the power of a lie.We live in a world full of them, and I'm embarrassed to admit how many times I've been deceived by them. Once, my wife and I watched a television show about how the United States faked the lunar landing. I was shocked! Horrified! For twenty-four hours I actually believed we never went to the moon. Another time, my friend Hayes invited me to this costume party he was throwing at his house Friday night. Guess what. It wasn't a costume party. Of course that had to be the time I dressed in my chicken suit. Not that I usually fall for that kind of stuff, it's just we fall for that kind of stuff all the time. Heck, when I was in high school, I believed a bowl cut actually made me look good!

What about you? What lies have you believed? What lies might you be believing right now?

∽

Jesus had been doing some serious ministry that day. From dawn to dusk, He had been healing people, telling stories and changing lives. It was evening now, and the crowds were still there. Folks were still clamoring for His attention. But Jesus was tired, and so were His disciples. A quiet boat ride across the lake would be just the kind of rest the doctor ordered. He motioned for the disciples to hop on board.[4]

In no time Jesus was in the back, fast asleep. Unfortunately for the disciples, sleep would not be in the cards for them. A furious squall came up out of nowhere, and before they knew what had hit them, gale force winds and white-capped waves were crashing over the sides of their tiny vessel. The boat was filling with water. The disciples were freaking out. Mind you, some of these guys were seasoned fishermen. They were used to crazy conditions. However, they also knew what a storm like this could mean: *death*. And there was Jesus in the back of the boat, sawing logs. "Teacher, do you not care that we are perishing?" shouted one of them between thunderclaps.[5]

I picture Jesus yawning, slowly uncurling from fetal position, smacking His lips and rubbing His eyes. Then, standing up, Scripture says, He "rebuked" the waves. Not sure what that means. Some kind of judo chop maybe. Whatever it was, it worked. The storm suddenly stopped. The lake turned to glass. The stars came out. And Jesus turned back to His disciples, their jaws dropped open, and He said, "Why are you so afraid?" I imagine Jesus cat-stretching, yawning, going back to sleep, and leaving the bewildered disciples saying to themselves: "Who then is this, that even the wind and the sea obey him?"[6]

But for these disciples, their adventure was far from over. Crossing to the other side of the lake, they landed in a region called Gerasenes where they were met by a monster. A human, actually. At least the guy was once human. Listen to the way Scripture describes him:

> He lived among the tombs. And no one could bind him anymore, not even with a chain, for he had often been bound with shackles and chains, but he wrenched the chains apart, and he broke the shackles in pieces. No one had the strength to subdue him. Night and day among the tombs and on the mountains he was always crying out and cutting himself with stones.[7]

Whoa. Maybe monster *is* a better way to describe him.

Well, guess who got out of the boat first? Jesus. That's right. Jesus, the Prince of Peace, stepped out of the boat to go toe-to-toe with the Gerasenes Monster. Now this is interesting to me. Scripture says that the man ran and fell on his knees, screaming: "What do you want with me, Jesus, Son of the Most High God? Swear to God that you won't torture me!"[8] How did this guy know who Jesus was? They had never met. And yet, the Gerasenes Monster knew more about Jesus than anybody Jesus had met thus far in the Gospel of Mark! Now this is even *more* interesting to me: We learn in the next verse that Jesus had been the first to speak.

"For Jesus *had* said to him, 'Come out of this man, you evil spirit!'"[9] You get that? It appears as if Jesus also *knew this guy*!

There is more to this story, but let me pause for a second to point out something astounding. Look at what Jesus does: He leaves thousands of people to cross a lake to meet a guy who is so feared and despised that his hometown, including his family, has exiled him to a graveyard. To get to him, Jesus fights not one but two potentially deadly circumstances: the first, a furious, boat-destroying-killer-of-a hurricane; the second, a Hulk-like man whose body has been taken over by a "Legion" of demons (more on Legion later, but do you know how big a "legion" is? "The organization of legions varied greatly over time but they were typically composed of up to 5,400 soldiers."[10]) Whoa. Five thousand-plus demons and Jesus doesn't flinch! Five thousand-plus demons and *they* fall at *His* feet! (*Who is this man?* is right!) Now, I'm getting ahead of myself, but check this out: Jesus destroys the demons, restores the guy to health, gets back in the boat, and returns back across the lake. You get that? Jesus faced all this adversity *for one guy*, for a guy that the world had completely written off. Jesus, on the other hand, loved him so much He put His own life on the line to save him. That's crazy. But as you get to know Jesus, you discover that He does this kind of thing all the time. It's His nature. Jesus hunts people down. I wouldn't be surprised if He's hunting you down this very moment!

Back to the story.

Who knows how the demons had taken possession of this man. Maybe he had let them in. Maybe he had been seduced by their power. Maybe he had bought into the lie that strength would get him the life he wanted. All we know is that the demons had taken up residence. And sure enough, they had given the man power, all right. However, the power came at a price. It had cost him his freedom. The man was strong, but he could only use it to abuse himself. He was alive but had been sentenced to live among the dead.

The demons were in control. Like Wormtongue stole Théoden's power to speak, the demons had done the same to this man. They had stolen everything. And it was the demons to whom Jesus was speaking now: "What is your name?" He asked.

"My name is Legion," came the reply, "for we are many"[11] (and at five thousand-plus. I'd say *many* is an understatement).

Now, when I picture this interaction between Jesus and Legion, I picture some scene out of a horror movie. It's harder for me to imagine this happening *for real*. Not that demons aren't real. I believe they are. However, demon possessions and exorcisms and matters like that simply are not part of my day-to-day experience. Don't know about you, but here is my sneaking suspicion: Even though you and I are not well acquainted with demons, I have the feeling that they are well acquainted with you and me. And here in this passage we learn *demons have names*.

Whether we recognize them or not, their lies are ceaselessly knocking on the doors of our souls, and when we listen—and we believe—they're in. They take up residence. Demons like the one named Lust. He tricks me into thinking that women are sex objects; he fools me into desiring pleasure over love. Sometimes it feels like he has totally taken over my eyes and my mind. Of course, he's not the only one. There is his sister named Negative Body Image. She doesn't just go after women any more. She attacked me in first grade when a girl classmate called me "bubble butt." I have been self-conscious about it ever since.

Then, there are the triplets named Bitterness, Resentment, and Unforgiveness. Many a relationship has been poisoned by this trio of evil. Mercilessly, they attack the hurting and the harmed. They hit people when they are down. They dig in their hooks where people feel most vulnerable. They tangle themselves into the fabric of the heart, making it nearly impossible to get them out. If only those demons were the only ones. Unfortunately, there are more. Like the demon named Mocked and the demon named Bullied and the demon called Depression and her big brother Suicidal. One of the worst demons is Shame. She overwhelms us like a cloak made of lead. She chains us to believe lesser things. She puts shackles on our freedom. Shame prevents us from believing that life can be any better than misery. I'll tell you, Shame is a demon like no other.

And there are *many* others—demons like the seven that history calls the "Deadly Sins"—Gluttony, Greed, Sloth, Wrath, Envy, Pride, and the aforementioned Lust. There are the demons named Deception, Betrayal, and Revenge. Oh, and Addiction, with his deadly disguises. He has the good old standbys of Drugs and Alcohol of course, but nowadays, Addiction has taken on dozens of forms, things like: Compulsive Aggression, Kleptomania, Pyromania, Gambling, Food, Sex, Pornography, Computers, Video Games, Working, Exercising, Religious Devotion, Pain, Cutting, and Shopping (according to one website).[12]

My name is Legion, for we are many.

Perhaps you and I are more acquainted with demons than we care to admit.

These evil spirits are the foot soldiers of Satan, and like soldiers they have been trained to destroy us, to kill us from the inside out as they slowly take possession of our lives.

And we let them in when we believe their lies. And I believe them all the time. When I over-exercise to compensate for how much I hate my body, when I cut myself because I feel so numb, or when I get drunk to make the pain go away—these are the signs, the symptoms, of a hostile takeover. It's what Imagine Dragons sing about: *Don't get too close / It's dark inside.*[13]

Yes, it's true. You and I are dark inside, aren't we?

When we turned our backs on God, which is what sin is, we opened ourselves to invasion. Ever since the fall of Adam and Eve, mankind has been suffering from Satan's constant attacks.

And we'd still be there if it weren't for Jesus.

He loved us too much to leave us in that state. Like Jesus did for this man in the graveyard. He battled hell and high water (literally, in the case of this man) to set us free.

Think about Jesus' words in the context of what we have just been studying:

"Truly, truly, I say to you, everyone who practices sin is a slave to sin. The slave does not remain in the house forever; the son remains forever. So if the Son sets you free, you will be free indeed."[14]

You hear Him? Jesus came to set you free.

So how do you become free? Great question, and it's very important to answer it right, especially because we find ourselves in the same reality that Théoden and the Gerasenes Monster found themselves in. We can't free ourselves. We might not have physical chains hanging from our wrists and ankles, but the chains might as well be there. Your soul has been taken prisoner, and there is a legion of demons standing guard over it. It feels like there is no way out, no escape. We can't change. Only Jesus can save us. Only He has the power to break us out of our prison lives.

And watch how He does it. Like Gandalf, Jesus doesn't mess around with Legion. As soon as He stepped out of the boat, He spoke: "Come out of the man!"[15] And the demons, powerful as they were, quaked in His presence. But Jesus wasn't satisfied with scare tactics. He took drastic measures. What kind of drastic measures? Well, He sent each member of Legion into a pig, then He sent the entire herd hurtling over a cliff into the sea, never to be heard from again.[16] Jesus acted quickly and decisively. Demons won't leave us alone if we treat them mildly, if we fight them halfheartedly. But when we let Jesus take control, watch out. All hell breaks loose. And true change can happen.

See what happens to Théoden once he is freed of the demonic Wormtongue:

Slowly, Théoden left his chair. A faint light grew in the hall again … with faltering steps the old man came down from the dais and paced softly through the hall. Wormtongue remained lying on the floor. They came to the door and Gandalf knocked.

"Open! he cried. "The Lord of the Mark comes forth!" … "Now, lord," said Gandalf, "look out upon your land! Breath the free air again!"

"It is not so dark here," said Théoden.

"No" said Gandalf. "Nor does age lie so heavily on your shoulders as some would have you think. Cast aside your prop!"

From the king's hand the black staff fell clattering on the stones. He drew himself up, slowly, as a man that is stiff from long bending over some dull toil. Now tall and straight he stood, and his eyes were blue as he looked into the open sky.

"Dark have been my dreams of late," he said, "but
I feel as one new-awakened."[17]

Théoden wakes from his nightmare and finds that he is younger and taller than he believed.

Now, check out what happens to the Gerasenes Monster: "[The herdsmen] came to Jesus and saw the demon-possessed man, the one who had the legion, sitting there, clothed and in his right mind."[18] The man was dressed (earlier, he must have been naked!). He was in his right mind (earlier, his mind had been clouded with lies). He was free. He begged to go with Jesus, but Jesus said to him, "Go home to your friends and tell them how much the Lord has done for you, and how he has had mercy on you." So he did and began to tell the story in Decapolis (which means Ten Cities), "and everyone marveled."[19]

That's great and all, but why did Jesus not allow the man to go with Him? It seems odd, doesn't it, that Jesus would send the man away? I thought Jesus was about relationships, and this guy was *begging* for one.

The answer is, I don't know. There are times when Jesus does allow the people He heals to follow Him.[20] For whatever reason, He instructs this man to go home. Maybe Jesus wanted this man and his family to be reunited. Maybe there was someone there who needed to hear his story. We do find out later that when Jesus returned to this region, people came running to Him with their sick.[21] So many people in fact, Jesus ended up feeding 4,000 men! (They just counted men. There would have been women and children there as well.) Could it be that Jesus used this outcast to reach the ten cities of Decapolis? Could be.

Who knows what Jesus might inspire you or me to do? Jesus has way bigger plans for us than we have for ourselves. Our job is to trust the process. To trust Him, and get His help to fight off the evil one and his too-easy-to-believe lies. Jesus puts it this way, and I'll let Him finish the chapter for us: "If you hold to my teaching, you are really my disciples. Then you will know the truth, and the truth will set you free."[22]

---

[1] J. R. R. Tolkien, *The Two Towers* (New York, New York; Ballantine Books, 1965), 148.

[2] Ibid., 149.

[3] Ibid., 151.

[4] These stories are found in Mark 4:35—5:20.

[5] Mark 4:38.

[6] Mark 4:39–41.

[7] Mark 5:3–5.

[8] Mark 5:6–7 (NIV 1984).

[9] Mark 5:8 (NIV 1984, emphasis added). Note that other translations, including the ESV, translate this as "was saying," not "had said."

[10] See http://en.wikipedia.org/wiki/Roman_legion.

[11] Mark 5:9.

[12] http://www.healthyplace.com/addictions/addictions-information/types-of-addiction-list-of-addictions/.

[13] "Demons" written by Imagine Dragons and Alex da Kid.

[14] John 8:34–36.

[15] Mark 5:8.

[16] See Mark 5:11–13. (Why did Jesus grant the demons' request? Why did He destroy people's livelihood in the process? Great questions. I honestly don't know.)

[17] Tolkien, 151–153.

[18] Mark 5:15.

[19] Mark 5:19–20.

[20] See Mark 10:46–52. Verse 52 says, "Immediately he recovered his sight and followed him on the way."

[21] Mark 7:31–32.

[22] John 8:31-32 (NIV 1984).

Study 5

You Were Made to Live

[Primary text: John 11:1–53]

Live? That's easy. I can do it in my sleep. Actually, I *do* do it in my sleep. I do it all the time. I do it without thinking about it. My heart's beating this very instant. I breathe whether I want to or not. I'm a natural. I live. I'm alive. I was born that way. And I will stay that way until the day I die.

Living is easy.

Oh, really?

If living is so easy, try it. Go ahead. Try to make something live. How about this book in your hand? See if you can get it to move on its own. Any luck? How about that cup on the table? Convince it to fill itself up. Or your shoe? Make it able to smell. (Oh, it *smells*, all right.) You get my point. *Living is not so easy when you are not alive.*

Ex nihilo is a Latin term meaning "out of nothing." For centuries, it has been used to describe the ability that God alone has: the ability to create life. Psalm 33:8 says that God spoke the universe into being and breathed the stars into existence. As a matter of fact, God used the same technique on us: "The LORD God formed the man of dust from the ground and *breathed* into his nostrils *the breath of life*, and the man became a *living* creature."[1] In other words, it may not be easy for you and me to bring something to life, but God can do it simply by exhaling!

If there is one thing we can say is true about God, we can say He is a Life-Giver. We wouldn't be here otherwise. In the same way, Jesus came to give us life.

Wait a second. I *am* alive, and the people Jesus hung out with were alive, too. So what kind of life did Jesus come to give us? Great question. And there is actually more than one answer to it. The first is this: When you were born, you were born with an incurable condition, one that would ultimately kill you. As a result, no matter how healthily you live, you will eventually die. This reality is not God's original design. He did not create us to live only for a little while. He created us to live forever. And God sent Jesus on a mission to make this forever-life possible for us.

The second way Jesus gives us life is described in one of His most often quoted sayings: "I came that they may have life and have it abundantly" (John 10:10b). We'll get to this abundant life in a few minutes. But first, it's important to note that this frequently quoted verse has another part to it. Here is the whole verse: "The thief comes only to steal and kill and destroy. I came that they may have life and have it abundantly" (John 10:10a).

Really? *Thief*? Who is Jesus talking about?

He is talking about an adversary, one who is not as strong as God; nevertheless, one who is still deadly. Who is he? Well, he goes by many names: the Lord of the Flies, the Ruler of the Kingdom of the Air, the Father of Lies, the Accuser, the Deceiver, the Devil, Satan. I'm guessing you've heard of him. Satan is God's enemy. And make no mistake, he is powerful and evil and hell-bent on inflicting as much pain on God as possible. But he can't do that directly. God is too strong for that. So Satan does the next best thing: he hurts what God loves, His creation. And tops on his list is you and me.

Satan hates you, and he uses anything at his disposal to steal, kill, and destroy you. Two thousand years ago when Jesus entered the scene, it appeared like Satan, the Evil One, was winning the war. The world was lost, incapable of saving itself. Here's the way Scripture puts it:

> You were dead in your transgressions and sins, in which you used to live when you followed the ways of this world and of the ruler of the kingdom of the air, the spirit who is now at work in those who are disobedient. All of us also lived among them at one time, gratifying the cravings of our flesh and following its desires and thoughts. Like the rest, we were by nature objects of wrath.[2]

In other words, when Jesus came, humanity was on death row. By choosing our way over God's way, mankind had condemned themselves by their actions. And there was nothing they could do about it. You and me included. That's right. You and I are in the same boat. Our hearts might be beating, but one day they will stop. What's worse, if there can be such a thing, our souls, which are eternal, will be sentenced to eternal death, which is what Scripture describes as hell.

That was the reality when Jesus entered the world. Humanity had turned their backs on God. Satan looked like he was in charge. And the world had become a very dark place. A war zone, actually. And when Jesus came as a baby, it was not clear which side was going to win. In fact, the odds seemed stacked against Him. Nevertheless Jesus accepted the mission anyway. Our souls were on the line. *So was His life.*

Fast-forward thirty-three years and we find Jesus well into His public ministry. Folks are getting healed. Demons are getting exorcised. And lives are being transformed by the love of a God who accepts them as they are. It must have been incredible to be alive back then—to be that close to God in the flesh. How could you not be changed? Jesus, the Life-Giver, was here! Yet at the same time, Jesus had this way of royally ticking off the people who didn't want things to change. Some of these people tried to kill Him, and eventually they succeeded.

~

In a village called Bethany, there was a family made up of two sisters and a brother. Mary, Martha, and Lazarus were their names. They were friends of Jesus. On different occasions, they had hosted Him and His disciples when they had come through town. This time, before Jesus and the disciples arrived, Lazarus had gotten really sick, so sick he died. By the time Jesus reached the village, Lazarus had been dead and buried four days.

And Mary and Martha were ticked. Martha was so upset she couldn't even wait until Jesus arrived before giving Him a piece of her mind. See, Martha knew who Jesus was. She had seen Him heal people. She knew Jesus could have saved her brother if He had wanted to. But He didn't. Why not? Lazarus was His friend! Martha knew Jesus didn't play favorites, but His willful inaction felt like a bit of a betrayal. (We learn earlier that Jesus was told that Lazarus was dying and yet He stayed two extra days where He was before traveling to see him.)[3]

You can imagine Martha fighting back tears as she said, "If you had been here, my brother would not have died."

"Your brother will rise again," said Jesus, kindly.

Martha answered, "I know that he will rise again in the resurrection on the last day." (Jews believed that the souls of men and women remained "sleeping" until the "last day" when God called them up to heaven.)

I picture Jesus placing His hand gently on her shoulder. "I am the resurrection and the life," He said. "Whoever believes in me, though he die, yet shall he live, and everyone who lives and believes in me shall never die. Do you believe this?"[4]

"I'm not sure what you're talking about, but I believe in you," she said (my translation). *What was Jesus talking about? Resurrection? Life? What does that mean?* It means this: Jesus' purpose was to bring the dead back to life.

I love how this verse in Hebrews puts it: "Since the children have flesh and blood, [Jesus] too shared in their humanity so that by his death he might destroy him who holds the power over death—that is, the devil—and free those who all their lives were held in slavery by their fear of death."[5]

When Jesus died on the cross, He suffered the consequence of our incurable condition; by doing so, He made a way for us to not suffer the consequence. In other words, He brought us, the dead, to life. That's what He means by resurrection.

But did you catch the first part of that verse? Jesus shared our humanity. Just like you and me, Jesus ate when He was hungry, He slept when He was tired, and He bled when He was cut. He laughed. He cried. He experienced everything you and I experience every day. He lived. He lived perfectly, but He felt everything you and I feel. Maybe more so. The word often used to describe Jesus' emotions is the Greek word *splanch-nizomai* (easy for *you* to say!). According to Thayer's Greek Lexicon, *splanchnizomai* means, "to be moved as to one's bowels."[6] How about that? Dealing with our crap made Jesus feel the same! Actually, that is not entirely what that word means. In fact, when the writers of Scripture used the word *splanchnizomai* they were trying to describe Jesus' compassion, His heart. But it was more than heart to the people who witnessed it. Jesus experienced people's pain physically. It was from the gut. Visceral. He felt so profoundly it was as if He absorbed others' pain into His actual body.

As a matter of fact, when Jesus saw the anguish of Mary, Martha's sister, He wept.[7]

Why is that important? It's important for a number of reasons. For one, Jesus feels what you are going through. He understands it so well He literally *feels* your pain. In Jesus, you have a Friend who will go with you through the struggle. That might be different than the Rescuer you want Him to be at times. But think how great it is to have a Comforter, someone who meets you in the middle of your mess. That's what Jesus does. He meets us. He does life *with* us. Do you get how amazing that is? Jesus didn't just give us life after death; Jesus wants us to experience life now.

I mentioned earlier that we would talk about abundant life. Well, here it is. Actually, here is what it is not: Abundant life is not a life where you are always happy and things always go your way. That is what we call fantasy. What Jesus offers is *real*.

Remember the progression from the Introduction? Get to know Jesus. Because the more you get to know Him, the more you will fall in love with Him. And the more you fall in love with Him, the more you will follow Him. And the more you follow Him, the more you will become like Him. And the more you become like Him, the more you become yourself. Remember that?

That's what this life is about. You see, when you get to know Jesus and fall in love with Him so madly you follow Him wherever He leads and the two of you get so close that you start resembling each other—you know what happens? It's crazy, but it's true: You start living in a way that feels totally brand new and totally natural all at the same time. Why? Because it's life the way it was meant to be lived. *With Jesus*. A life with Him is the life you were made to live!

This quote gets to what I'm getting at:

Life is an opportunity, benefit from it. Life is beauty, admire it. Life is bliss, taste it. Life is a dream, realize

it. Life is a challenge, meet it. Life is a duty, complete
it. Life is a game, play it. Life is a promise, fulfill it. Life
is sorrow, overcome it. Life is a song, sing it. Life is a
struggle, accept it. Life is a tragedy, confront it. Life is
an adventure, dare it. Life is luck, make it. Life is too
precious, do not destroy it. Life is life, fight for it.[8]

In other words, life gives us all kinds of things. It's true.
Life gives us things. Whether we see those things as
gifts or burdens has a lot to do with what we believe
about the Giver. And how we respond to those gifts
says a lot about what we believe about ourselves. Jesus
came to help us experience abundant life no matter the
circumstance. How? By meeting us where we are.

Jesus met Mary in her pain. He wept. He wept so
hard the people marveled at how He loved this family.[9]
But He didn't stop there; Jesus moved toward the tomb
of His friend. "Take away the stone!" He shouted. (The
tomb was a cave enclosed by a heavy stone, similar in
design to the one where Jesus would be buried.)

A murmur went through the crowd.

"By this time there will be an odor," whispered Mary
to Jesus, "for he has been dead four days."[10] But Jesus
insisted that the tomb be opened anyway. Odor or not,
He wanted to see His friend.

So they rolled away the stone, and after Jesus said a prayer, He shouted: "Lazarus, come out!"

And guess what? Lazarus did. He walked out dressed like a mummy. Ha! Can you imagine what happened next? I bet you can. The place went berserk. People started putting their faith in Jesus left and right. But not all of them. Those who were against Jesus felt more threatened than ever. They said, "If we let [Jesus] go on like this, everyone will believe in him, and the Romans will come and take away both our place and our nation."[11] And place and nation were important to them. "So from that day on they made plans to put [Jesus] to death."[12]

Like I said, Jesus entered a war zone.

One more thing about resurrection before we move on: Resurrection means to bring something dead back to life. So in order for something to be resurrected, there is something that must first happen to it. You get it? It has to die. In order for Jesus to resurrect Lazarus, Lazarus had to be dead. The same was true for what God let happen to His Son. And the same is true for you. Jesus came to resurrect you, which means that first you have to die! Now stay with me, because this is deep. Sometimes Jesus is going to allow things in your life to die—important things, things that matter, things like dreams, hopes, and relationships. Jesus is going to let things die in your life in order to give you back something even greater. This has happened to me more than once. My wife is a constant reminder. You see, if Jesus hadn't put to death some of my past relationships, I would never have the gift that Lia is to me. You might have some resurrection stories from your own life as well.

If not, you will.

Because Jesus is in the resurrection business. But Jesus' resurrection power came at a high price. It cost Jesus *His* life. Back to that Hebrews verse: *by His death* Jesus destroyed the one who held power over death.[13]

On the cross, Jesus fought the battle over life and death and won. Three days later, He proved it by coming back from the dead. And here's the best news: He will do the same for us! "For as by a man came death, by a man has come also the resurrection of the dead. For as in Adam all die, so also in Christ shall all be made alive."[14]

Don't overlook how amazing that is. Remember the passage from Ephesians we looked at earlier? It put our situation bluntly: "you were dead." And living is not so easy when you are not alive, am I right? But check out what the passage says next: "But because of his great love for us, God, who is rich in mercy, *made us alive* with Christ even when we were dead in transgressions—it is by grace you have been saved."[15] *Saved by grace*. You might have heard those words before. What do they mean? Simply this: You were given something you could not earn and did not deserve. What was it? Life. The Life-Giver gave you life. Why? So *you could live!*

The same passage in Ephesians ends with this sentence: "For we are God's workmanship, created in Christ Jesus to do good works, which God prepared in advance for us to do."[16] God, the Creator, has been working on us since before we were born. Now, the word "workmanship" might give some of you the image of a God with a hammer and chisel who is hacking away at you until He has made you into a desk or chair. But check this out: The word the writer uses here that has been translated "workmanship" is the Greek word *poiēma*. Do you see it? It's the word that became our English word "poem."

In a very true sense, God is writing a story with your life. No, even better, He's writing a *poem* with your life. And like all great literature, your poem will be full of adventure, intrigue, joy, and sorrow. There will be times of celebration and times of mourning. At points, God's poem will make those who experience it want to laugh, sing, dance, and cry. But no matter what happens, because of Jesus, you can know this for certain: Your poem will end well. For in Jesus, death does not get the last word. In fact, when you give the pages of your life over to Jesus, you'll discover your story ends with the very words that have been bestowed upon all the best stories ever told: happily ever after.

---

[1] Genesis 2:7, emphasis mine.

[2] Ephesians 2:1–3 (NIV 1984).

[3] See John 11:6.

[4] See John 11:23–26.

[5] Hebrews 2:14–15 (NIV 1984).

[6] See Strong's Concordance or online at www.blueletter-bible.org/lang/lexicon/lexicon.cfm?strongs=G4697.

[7] "Jesus wept" (John 11:35; the shortest verse in the Bible).

[8] The source of this quote is unknown to me. It is often attributed to Mother Teresa, however the website motherte-resa.org/08_info/Quotesf.html claims she never said it.

[9] See John 11:36.

[10] John 11:39.

[11] John 11:48.

[12] John 11:53.

[13] Hebrews 2:14. See also 1 Corinthians 15:54b–57.

[14] 1 Corinthians 15:21–22.

[15] Ephesians 2:4–5 (NIV 1984, my emphasis).

[16] Ephesians 2:10 (NIV 1984).

You Were Made To Make A Difference

[Primary text: Matthew 28:16–20]

"Now the eleven disciples went to Galilee, to the mountain to which Jesus had directed them. And when they saw him they worshiped him, but some doubted."[1]

They met Jesus on the mountain. Eleven of them. Judas wasn't there because, tragically, he had killed himself after betraying Jesus. The rest of the twelve had fled. Gone into hiding. Now there was news Jesus had come back to life. Shocking to say the least. But not exactly surprising. No less than three times, Jesus had predicted this precise thing would happen.[2] Now, women were reporting that they had spoken with

Him. In fact, the disciples were here on this mountain because that was where Jesus had told these women He wanted to meet them.

So here they were, and so was He. It must have been surreal, to see with their own eyes a person they had seen, days earlier, crucified. Jesus had been tortured beyond imagination, flogged within an inch of His life. Nail-like thorns had been jammed into His head. Actual nails had been hammered through His flesh. A spear had been thrust into His side. Everything but the spear had been meant to produce pain. The spear was to ensure death. You see, Jesus didn't die from the thorns or the nails; Jesus died by suffocation. He had become so weak he had become unable to breath.

Afterward, His body had been carried to a tomb carved out of rock. A boulder had been rolled in front of the entrance. It was too heavy to be removed by a single person, and the Romans had placed guards on duty to make sure no one even tried.

They had killed Him to stop a riot. They needed Him to stay that way lest He start a revolution. But they failed. The dead man rose. The rock rolled away. And the revolution continues to this day.

But the revolution hadn't started quite yet. Jesus' plan involved the disciples. He would provide the spark, but He was counting on them to carry His light to the world. Would they do it? Would His followers follow through? First, they would have to believe.

And *some doubted.*

Some doubted? How is that possible? How could they witness blind people seeing, deaf people hearing, mute people speaking, and doubt His power? How could they watch Jesus deliver people from demons and evil spirits and doubt His authority? How could they listen to Jesus talk about God so profoundly and so intimately and doubt His understanding? How could they see Jesus raise people from the dead and doubt He was God? And here He was now, standing directly in front of them, once dead, now alive! Only God could do something like that.

But some doubted.

It's hard to imagine. And yet, they did. Why? Well, I have a theory, and here it is: I don't think their doubt had anything to do about who Jesus was. After three years of miracles and wonders and teaching up close, I don't think it was possible to not believe in Him. The problem was believing in themselves. They couldn't get over it. Why would the one and only Son of God, Creator and King of everything, choose people like Peter, Andrew, and John to be His inner circle? It didn't make sense. It doesn't make sense, frankly. When God could have chosen anybody, why did He choose this bunch of misfits? Think about it. Jesus could have chosen the twelve most powerful people of His time. He could have chosen influencers. Or religious types, folks who knew the Scriptures and had credibility. He could have chosen popular folks, people who could give Him street cred. People who had connections. People who were at least attractive. Or nice. Instead, Jesus had chosen *them*: a few gnarly fishermen, a despised tax collector, a fringe-of-society zealot, and the rest of them nobodies. The writer Brennan Manning called them ragamuffins. You can call them what you want. They were *losers*. And they knew it.

Why would God choose *them*? Why would Jesus trust His message *to them*? It was too much for some of them to get over. And yet, Jesus was standing right there before them. The dead man was alive after completing everything He had set out to do. All He was asking from them was to believe it. Still, it was hard, even if there was no denying the fact. Jesus was alive. He had just shaken Philip's hand. He had just given James a fist bump. And whether the doubters were ready to receive it or not, Jesus was about to deliver the greatest commission ever given to anybody in history.

He said to them:

"All authority in heaven and on earth has been given to me. Go therefore and make disciples of all nations, baptizing them in the name of the Father and of the Son and of the Holy Spirit, teaching them to observe all that I have commanded you. And behold, I am with you always, to the end of the age."[3]

Clearly, Jesus believed in these men. Maybe that doesn't seem astonishing to you. After all, we know these guys as the great men they became. But you have to remember these disciples didn't start out that way. Take Peter for example. Peter was Jesus' closest friend. Just three days previously, Peter had denied even knowing Him. Now, Jesus was giving him marching orders to change the world! What was Jesus thinking? That must have been what was going through the disciples' minds. *We aren't cut out for this. Jesus, don't you remember when we ran for our lives at the sight of first blood?* And here was Jesus telling them to go to war for Him. He was making His deserters His generals!

Jesus, are you crazy?

I wonder if John thought about that line Jesus had told them a few months earlier: "Truly, truly, I say to you, whoever believes in me will also do the works that I do; and greater works than these will he do, because I am going to the Father."[4] It was one of those lines that Jesus just floated out there. Greater things than healings? Greater things than resurrections? There's no way. Jesus was Jesus. They were ... they were ordinary people.

You know, that's the challenge isn't it? It's not believing in God, necessarily; it's what you believe about yourself that makes following Him so hard. That was what the disciples struggled with. And it's the same thing you and I struggle with, too. We believe in God. But we don't believe that God can do anything about our stuff. We doubt God can change us or use us. We doubt the world can really be a better place. And we don't act like we think that what we do really matters. We don't believe it, not because we doubt God—we don't believe it because we doubt ourselves.

The truth is, God believes in you more than you believe in yourself. Now, that is a crazy thought, especially when you consider how awful God *knows* you are. He actually knows more about your junk than you do. And still He hasn't given up on you. He wants to use you. I mean that in the very best way. You are useful to God. When He created you, He gave you unique skills and attributes so that you could make a unique impact for Him. That's His purpose for you. He made you to make a difference.

Of course, God made you to be loved. Yes, God made you to belong. Yes, God made you to be free and to be whole and to live life fully. Ultimately, His purpose is for you to know Him, to have a forever relationship with Him. All that is true. But that isn't all. *God made you to live out His mission.*

Jesus came to save the world and every person in it. And there are people only you will be able to reach. Maybe it's your friend. Maybe it's a stranger. Maybe it's your parents, a sibling, a relative. But there are people that you will come in contact with who need to know Jesus—and *you* have the chance to be the one to introduce them.

Do you get it? You can't save them. You can't free them. You can't make them whole. But Jesus can, and *only* Jesus can. It's important to remember that. There will only ever be one Savior, and that's Jesus. Your job is to make the introduction, to pay attention to what Jesus is doing, and participate in it.

What's He doing? He's rescuing the world from the forces of evil. Someone is getting bullied. Stick up for her. A friend is making destructive decisions. Fight for him. Your sister doesn't know Jesus. Introduce them. God has you where you are for a reason. You are here to make a difference.

Why me? Why can't God use someone better qualified? Oh, He will. He will also use people *less* qualified, as a matter of fact. All Jesus needs is a willing participant.

But I don't know what I'm doing?

That's all right. You'll learn. There are techniques you can pick up (looks like we have a topic for another book). However, you have the most effective tool already. YOU. YOU HAVE A STORY. And the best thing you can do for Jesus is to share that story with others.

Wait. What? I don't have a story. Sure you do! Everyone does. And yours is going to make a huge impact as long as you share it. If you think about it, that's what the Bible is: people sharing their stories about their journeys with God.

It's really not that complicated. That's what makes it so meaningful and profound. People can debate ideas. But no one can deny a personal account. Allow me to share a bit of mine.

I was signed up to go to Young Life camp after my senior year of high school. For those of you unfamiliar with Young Life's camping program, its purpose is to introduce high school kids to Christ, but Jesus managed to change my life the night before I went to Young Life camp. You're not reading wrong—the night *before* I went to Young Life camp. That evening, a friend of mine called me to tell me that our Young Life leader did not want me to go. (I'm not making this up—my leader didn't want me to go to camp!) He said that he thought I was a bad influence (which was true). He didn't want me to be a distraction to the folks who were actually interested in finding out about Jesus. Wow!

Guess how I felt about that.

I'm not sure I can write it. Let's just say that the words I shouted at my friend on the other end of the line should never be repeated. I was infuriated. I told my friend that I would see him *and* our Young Life leader at the bus the next morning whether they liked it or not. Then, I hung up the phone. My mom gave me a *What was that all about?* look. I didn't think I could tell her without incriminating myself, so I kept my mouth shut. I went to bed. It was early, but the conversation had left me feeling tired.

Let me explain some things. God had been a part of my life from the beginning. My parents were committed. So was my sister. We went to church every Sunday. They loved it. To tell you the truth, I didn't think church was all that bad either. I just didn't let the God stuff stick around with me the rest of the week. To me, Jesus was a party-pooper, and I liked to party. Jesus cramped my style, or at least He'd make me feel guilty about it, and I didn't like feeling guilty. And I didn't, as long as I kept the God part of my life in a box.

I would let Him out on Sunday mornings and maybe again at Campaigners (Young Life's Bible study) or at the church youth group. In those places, it was OK to talk about having a relationship with Jesus. And the truth was, I wanted one.

Just not all the time. I wanted a relationship when it was convenient and safe and encouraged. I was afraid to bring God into the rest of my life. My friends might not like me anymore. And Jesus might not like the things I was doing.

I was really looking forward to Young Life camp. Young Life was fun, and at camp I could talk about God and not be afraid about what others might think. True, that afternoon I had hosted a party with a bunch of the guys who were going on the trip. True, we had gotten drunk. But that was then. I could still be the Christian Young Life guy tomorrow.

That was why my Young Life leader didn't want me to go. I was telling these younger guys through my actions that it was cool to follow Jesus on your own terms. Our leader didn't like that message. He didn't like it because it wasn't true.

I was lying in bed when I finally realized it. Staring up at the ceiling with my hands behind my head, it suddenly dawned on me: Following Jesus was an all or nothing proposition. There was no halfway or part of the time. Either I was all in or not at all.

My heart hurt to think about it because I loved Jesus. I just didn't like the idea of following Him all the time. I didn't like the rules that I thought I'd have to obey. I didn't want to stop the partying. I didn't want to stop treating girls the way I had been treating them. I knew that if I put Jesus first, things would have to change. But I didn't want to change. To be honest, I doubted if I could. I was addicted. I was addicted to my friends. I was addicted to girls. I was probably addicted to alcohol. If going all-in meant giving up my stuff, well, the thing I would have to give up was Jesus. He seemed to be the easier of the two to let go of. I was in too deep.

That's what I told Jesus, lying there on the bed staring up at the ceiling with my hands behind my head. "I can't change," I said. There were tears in my eyes. "So I guess this is good-bye."

I closed my wet eyes and fell asleep, the last thought in my head being that I had just erased my name out of the Book of Life. I was going to hell. And God would never want anything to do with me again.

And that's how I thought my life would stay. Except it didn't.

I'm not sure when it happened—or how or what, for that matter—but the next morning, I woke up a changed person. Sometime while I was sleeping, God had taken all those desires for other things and had replaced those desires with Himself. Actually, the desires didn't change. What changed was how I knew they were finally going to be satisfied. Does that make sense? It was seven o'clock in the morning, but I knew I wasn't going to drink again. I knew there were going to be hundreds of cute girls at camp, but suddenly the only person I wanted to love or have love me was Jesus. I didn't care what my friends thought. I didn't even care that my Young Life leader gave me the I-don't-believe-a-word-of-it look when I told him I was different. I was so happy, none of it mattered. Only Jesus did.

Let me tell you: That week at Young Life camp was the best week of my life. I had so much fun. And the best part was that everything God began the night before camp became more of a reality.

When I got home, there was a message from a friend of mine. His parents were out of town so he was having some people over. I went. On the way, I picked up a six-pack of Dr Pepper. I drank it while my friends were drinking what, a week ago, I would have been drinking. And you know what? I didn't miss it. I had a better time without it. As the night rolled on, I told my friends about the change that was going on inside of me. None of them believed it. One of the guys bet me one hundred bucks I would be drinking again within two weeks. I never cashed in on that bet. But I could have.

I was totally different.

A month later I went to college and I met all these amazing people who loved Jesus too. I became a Young Life leader and started sharing my story with high school guys. People started meeting Jesus for themselves. It was nuts. Six months earlier I was lost. Now, I was helping others get found.

That's the power of Jesus.

And the same power that He gave me, He has given you. All you have to do is believe it and act on it. Now, I must warn you. When you do, watch out. Because before you know it, Jesus is going to show up big time in your life, and you and your friends and your school and your town and the world will never be the same. Because you were made to make a difference, whether you believe you can or not. And you can, and you will, even if you struggle, even if you doubt, *because God believes in you!*

Oh my goodness, there is so much more I could say. But instead of giving you more to think about, let me remind you of what has already been said: You matter to God. And because you matter to God, He is committed to making you into the person He created you to be.

You have wounds. He will heal them.

You have made mistakes. He will forgive them.

You have hurt yourself and others. He will restore the things you have lost.

Not only that, out of the pain of your past God will make new and beautiful things.[5] He will help you become whole. He will give you a place to belong. He will love you with a love that will never let go of you. He will free you from every prison you find yourself in, every chain you get shackled to. He will give you life.

You see, God doesn't break us down. God breaks us open. Out of the hard shell, a shoot bursts forth and grows and flourishes and produces fruit. That is what God means for you. He wants you to grow and flourish and bless others with what He produces through you.

How? By getting to know Him. Jesus describes the relationship He wants with you to be like the relationship a tree has with its branches. He says this: "I am the vine; you are the branches. If a man remains in me and I in him, he will bear much fruit; apart from me you can do nothing."[6]

That's the key to life—knowing Jesus. Because the more you get to know Him, the more you will love Him.[7] And the more you love Him, the more you will follow Him.[8] And the more you follow Him, the more you will become like Him. And the more you become like Him, the more you become yourself.[9] And there is no other thing you were made for. You were made to become YOU. The real you. And with Jesus—and only with Him—that's exactly who you will become!

---

[1] Matthew 28:16–17.

[2] Matthew 20:17–19: "And as Jesus was going up to Jerusalem, he took the twelve disciples aside, and on the way he said to them, 'See, we are going up to Jerusalem. And the Son of Man will be delivered over to the chief priests and scribes, and they will condemn him to death and deliver him over to the Gentiles to be mocked and flogged and crucified, and he will be raised on the third day.'" Pretty specific, wouldn't you say? See also Matthew 16:21 and 17:22–23.

[3] Matthew 28:18–20.

[4] John 14:12.

[5] See Isaiah 61:3.

6 John 15:5 (NIV 1984).
7 John 15:9.
8 John 15:10.
9 John 15:10–11.

About the Author

Ned Erickson lives in Winston-Salem, North Carolina, with his wife, two kids, two dogs, six chickens, three hamsters, one turtle, and a fish. He is the author of *Falling Into Love* as well as the novel *Clay*, and has worked for Young Life for many years in a variety of roles. For more information visit his website: www.nederickson.com. Ned can be reached through the publisher at ran@whitecapsmedia.com.

Colophon

Book designed by Randolph McMann for Whitecaps Media

Main body composed in Chaparral Pro Regular 10.5/15. Chaparral Pro was created by Adobe designer Carol Twombly

Cover designed by Stephanie W. Dicken

426 Series editor: Kit Sublett

Be sure to visit
whitecapsmedia.com
for more
426 Series Bible studies
and the Study Guide
for this book

www.ingramcontent.com/pod-product-compliance
Lightning Source LLC
Chambersburg PA
CBHW060341050426
42449CB00011B/2810